Life Has Become More Cheerful

Also by Aidan Semmens

A Stone Dog
The Book of Isaac
Uncertain Measures

Aidan Semmens

Life Has Become More Cheerful

Shearsman Books

First published in the United Kingdom in 2017 by
Shearsman Books
50 Westons Hill Drive
Emersons Green
BRISTOL
BS16 7DF

Shearsman Books Ltd Registered Office
30–31 St. James Place, Mangotsfield, Bristol BS16 9JB
(this address not for correspondence)

www.shearsman.com

ISBN 978-1-84861-553-3

Copyright © Aidan Semmens, 2017.

The right of Aidan Semmens to be identified as the author
of this work has been asserted by him in accordance with the
Copyrights, Designs and Patents Act of 1988.
All rights reserved.

ACKNOWLEDGEMENTS
Thanks are due to the editors of the following magazines, in which some of
these poems, earlier versions or parts of them, have appeared:
*Blackbox Manifold, Free Verse, In Suffolk, Litmus, Long Poem Magazine,
Molly Bloom, Noon, Otoliths, Shearsman, Tears in the Fence, Under The Radar.*

Contents

I The Book of Revolution

1917	11
A Literate People Lives Happily	12
Poor Realm	13
Dead Souls	15
Dreams	16
The Redistribution of Joy	18
A Summary of Events Connected	20
A Testament So Toxic	23
Avant-Gardists in the Service of the Proletariat	26
The Glamour of Government, the Ecstasy of Power	28
The Pianist of Petrograd	30
On Suspicion of Sabotage in Project Planning	32
The Utensil is Good But the Soup is Bad	33
The House of the Gramophone Record, The House of the Book	34
Expert Witness	36
From the Directory of 1936	38
And Tonight the Hideous Angels Sue for Peace	42
Great Man Theory	43
Say Some of Your Poems to Me Again, Comrade Poet	45
The Passing of Boris Pasternak	49

II From the Aesthetics Bureau

Document 1	53
Leica Rangefinder, 50mm	60
I Could Tell You But Then You Would Have to Be Destroyed	62
Monochromatic	64
Visiting Time	65
Bleed	66
Purity	67
On Prenzlauer Allee	68

Child #98	69
Vision of Ezekiel	72
De Triomf van de Dood	74
The Garden of Earthly Delights	77
Unified Field Theory	79
News of the World	85
To Answer a Different Question Than the One Asked	86
Hut	87

III Stories About the Wind

In the Operations Room	91
Ghosts	92
Test Site III	93
Krasnogorskiy	95
Test Site IV: New Fire	100
Select Bibliography	102

Life is much better, comrades. Life has become more cheerful

—Joseph Stalin, 1938

I

The Book of Revolution

1917

Blessed is he that readeth, and they that hear the words of this prophecy, and keep those things which are written therein: for the time is at hand

this evening the atmosphere in the streets
as if the buildings themselves
the bedding roadway's earth
can feel and receive the smell
interpret moments of great significance
by corner and storeway entrances the people are seized

onlooking, listening, the alarm signal
knot of friends and stranger
bright faces mobile, earnest and a few frightened
of unknown quantities, expect unexpectedly
wild estimates, the discussed theories
the turning of heads to the tones down roads

empty other but all observers
a little children, current running
but roaring that resounds in the far canyons
and the urban watercourse
is not fire from the throats of children
or survey, call the shots which thunder

rattle windows, poverty-stricken restless
shudders nerve
the anxious and enthralled
child's eye wants to know and surprised
which a woman shining
although perhaps only reflects

A Literate People Lives Happily

And I wept much, because no man was found worthy
to open and to read the book

in the central kolkhoz market
the peasants come to sell
their produce to the workers of the town
fruits, tubers, bulbs carefully weighed
all sorts of unexpected goods
may suddenly appear in the shops

in the Kharkov Palace of Industry
a bare rectangular functionality
coexists with an exuberance
of heights, form and regular windows
just as you heard the timber
of the previous edifice give loud cracks

a class in the liquidation of illiteracy
is in progress, empty faces turned
to the reader of documents
formerly deemed fatally toxic

there will be no burning of books:
it is better economics to pulp them
for printing again with better words

Poor Realm

> *Soon the enlightened nations will put on trial those who have hitherto ruled over them. The kings shall flee into the deserts, into the company of the wild beasts whom they resemble; and Nature shall resume her rights*
> —Saint-Just, 1793

ring tocsin
calls to revolt
trumpetcall awakes
from slaves everywhere

fashioning wonders, faith
in plots and conspiracies –
provision of bread
certifies public order

infinite happiness will lead
from this anywhere,
the end of injustice, war,
conflict and shipping

the raised question is that persons
would dare to think,
people's knowledge acquired
finally to bring revolution

the spirit of moderation is to be expunged
armies launched against speculation
and greed, patriotic
of rural areas

an army that could work
to eradicate and punish the traitor,
monopolists, moderates, peaceful
innocents, all sorts of cold and suspect

war in castles
peace in the cottage
priests forced oath of hatred
– *pauvre paysan, pauvre royaume*

farmer is not sufficiently engaged
to accept the blood sacrifice
their son, the evil that besets us
that we do not have government

republican terrorist past infection
dechristianisation or democratic
watch committees scrutinize
foreigners and suspected activities

what fruit is plucked
from the tree of liberty?
what right of equality
until his own property be abolished?

unordered more
unattended more
time comes to end
dying of hunger and cold

Dead Souls

In the sweat of thy face shalt thou eat bread
—Genesis 3:19

it's no use being too clever
a man who works on the land
is purer, nobler, the factories
will come into being by themselves
I am afraid I shall move to the town
which ends in gambling and drunkenness
one may buy a library of books
and never read them a shadow
of gloomy black melancholy – here
the manuscript breaks off
for two pages a damp
dank cell reeking of soldiers' boots
a voice echoing in hollow distance

Dreams

> *Thy merchants were the great men of the earth;*
> *for by thy sorceries were all nations deceived*

awake, awake, utter a song
a bitter wind blowing from
Paradise, the end of order

in dream time we plot
the fall of autocrats
and it need not be in play
a good bomb well served
will do it nicely –
by whose authority
is it forbidden
but by theirs
we do not recognise?

thou shouldst not kill
– but they do
impoverish or imprison
– but they do
torture or sow fear
as they do

we fast, our wives
are made widows
the compact roll of portable memory
carried through the fires of disaster

those days before the revolution
were glorious days – days of struggle,
of romance and heroism, fervour,
bright hopes and pristine thought,
a vision of dignity and justice

the destruction of the unjust regime
is but one necessary step

there is no greater poison than power
but someone must take it

The Redistribution of Joy

> *I have lived a dissipated life but loved goodness*
> —Dostoevsky, *The Brothers Karamazov*

look at the book, comrade
it is written in the book
I suddenly see a new self
far removed from previous
troubles and vanity
if I have a defect
it is that I am not always
sufficiently cheerful
and self-confident

we must have colourful fabric
with cheerful patterns
associated with the revolutionary spirit
dress reform and thought unity
society reordered
with the virtuous at the summit

technocracy and money-grubbing
will give way to the reign of virtue
when people work for the good of all

if I wanted to work for the democracies
how would I know what to do?
who knows what the strategy
and tactics of Wall Street are?

we are advanced people
we want to lead a cultural life
we want bicycles, pianos
phonographs, records, radio sets
there are still many administrative workers

and former people
who travel about in cars

here on the industrial front
we must also have heroism
the mountain has crushed man like a frog –
we must shove the mountain
back into place

A Summary of Events Connected

For the great day of his wrath is come; and who shall be able to stand?

we are all of us at risk
the siren call can come
at any time

the banality we elevate
is the thing most inevitable
in every life

the art bought or ransacked
in the name of the emperor
belongs now to the people

yet the unbearable randomness
of political agitation increases
the preponderance of madmen

there are many maps and only one
has any meaning
among these shattered walls

here lies an unknown man
who had not quite escaped
caught between dependence and disgust

turning tricks in a shattered city
a lunar land with barely
a stone standing

several wooden notebooks survive
anecdotes about fear
and intimacy with the illustrious dead

Heracles found no flavour in the classics
preferring Adventures in Cookery
a text now lost

when Linus tried to show him
the error of his taste
he beat him to death with a chair leg

a visitor to Alexandria disembarked
to a babble of strange tongues
on a quayside lined with sphinxes

material inheritance of inscrutable structures
the threatening allure of foreign plays
all those parodies of tragedy

India was now much closer
Alexander reached the Punjab
and Egypt traded with the Deccan

road trip romances enact
anxiety of immigrants and their dread
of the conquered foreigner

the slow reveal of the photograph
developing clarity from fog
oblique drama of quiet reflection

on ruined houses in a flooded plain
here and there pieces of plaster
or a leaning wheel

hats and oaks and elms and china
plates silvered with the effects
of primitive chromatography

we must stay ahead of surveillance technology
to keep our citizens safe
confine as lunatics enemies of the state

a burst of violence
in the interests of wellbeing –
I feel much better since the revolution

A Testament So Toxic

Translations from The Book of Isaac

I

here it is, finally got here, the best flour!
we push on further but can find nowhere to work
the room is empty, a telephone on a desk
cases of shells, revolvers, machinegun belts
others have stacked their arms and sat on the floor
supping tea from mugs, salt herrings and crusts of bread
like passengers huddled together in railway stations
a reek of greatcoats and boots, a savage draught
while others with hopeless shrugs jostle their way
in streets made slippery with trodden mud and snow
many regiments fought the enemy within
uncertain exactly who that foe might be
I was told that work was rapidly going ahead
while others, with sceptical smiles, told another tale

II

those days before the revolution were glorious days
days of struggle, romance and heroism
fervour, bright hopes and most positive thought
a vision of dignity, justice for all –
the destruction of the brutal tsarist regime
was but one necessary step towards
the socialist utopia of which we dream;
ah, pessimist, you do not know the people
crowds on the Nevski are bigger today than ever
his sentences cracked like whips and cut as deep
the cavalry attacked and were in turn assaulted
– ah, pharaohs, your end is coming! we're here to destroy
fresh blood on the paving, two bodies, a falling man
from where we stood we could see the red fires' glow

III

for the passéists among us, great Apollo
has hoist a glaring sun above the streets,
the Poets' Café, monument to us all
where a Mauser lies beside a plate of cakes –
doesn't it make you happy to feel free?
the king of clowns is fond of pregnant men
in a city of swollen breasts and horses' rumps
too much seems still unfamiliar and unclear
as still we consider the riddles of the sphinx
singers with voices too powerful for the room
dancers not dressed to dance, an orange wall
before which he sits with red scarf neatly knotted
demented squares battle with rhomboids on
the peeling façades of colonnaded villas

IV

the cellar steps, the greasy light, the sweat
breathed in and out of stained and clammy walls
the functionary's pale and pustular flesh
oozing from his collar, stiffly eased
by sausage fingers probing in the cleft
stuffed uniform bulging like the padded door
of a soundproofed cell, a chintzy underground
neurosis for the apparatchik's healing
microphones are buried, set in stone
where queasy revelations may amuse
the listener but it's still a dreary game
performance of a wayward giftless prophet:
abrade the pavings, underpin the blocks
that shift and threaten in a tottering state

V

we have cast down the tsar and subjected ourselves to these…
no one gives us salvation, not heroes nor gods; the people
will stand like a wall in defence of their holy things
the ikons, the vestments, gold chalices, paper wings
for flights into fancy without drab need of boots
the ground is fully prepared for insurrection
not ploughed or tilled or sown for growing food
but only for the bloody resurrection
of fighting men and under-trodden women –
in the wood the mushrooms are out in plenty
bare cups raised up to bear the gift of rain
a girl-child squats to examine the waxy fruit
observe the nameless busy insects, hear
the jays at battle with the crows above

Avant-Gardists in the Service of the Proletariat

The artists' palette is the street – Mayakovsky

and, Vladimir Vladimirovich, if I may
perhaps the windswept steppes and forest too
the dinted cornfield
and collective farm –
not giant bogatyrs but peasants now
bestride the land, dwarfing
the trees and distant mills
turning and weaving
useful objects for the new society

faceless, like the looming planes
and airships over palaces
they become geometric abstracts
a woman with a saw
might be holding bunting
or a decorative linen sash

Molodtsova stares back
arms folded, scarf tied neatly
a shockworker stilled
by chickens scratching
by factory walls
before a horse in shafts
beneath a blossoming tree

the new Jerusalem is a shattered
shrine in a forest
brightly coloured onion domes
set at crazy angles
awaiting the wrecking-ball

icons of the new Russia
a madonna and child posed

above blue-painted walls
of an elegant capital
a tram conductor's
a goddess lit
by electrical flashes, power
of Elijah and Zeus
stretching for the sunlight
of a golden future only just
out of reach, a question
not of style but of commitment

with or without metaphysics
there will be constructive
sculptural forms of furniture
employing no incantations
images to fuel the new myths
blighted as they may be
by hidden meanings
encouraging interpretation

we will make it the way it is
and it will not be what you need
similarity to realism will not save us
until the style of the new epoch
becomes clear – the new hero
not a person but a people
or a class of people, overcoming weakness
of character and flesh, social material
within a shared forcefield
a formula superceding
all the elements of nature

heads as of wood or stone become
components in an intricate design
your peasant is not so interested
in suprematism or form –
but please do not gossip, the deceased
dislike that sort of thing terribly

The Glamour of Government, the Ecstasy of Power

the time for words is past, events
do not form themselves into a picture

insurrection is an art
and like all arts it has its laws

the extent of sacrifice matters little
what counts is the greatness of the goal

we cannot go back
but we are not going forward very far

the heroic era is past
we are slaves of the myriad dead

information from paper smells of paper
but a soldier is an absurd person

here I am expecting a trainload of ammunition
and they send me a trainload of priests

apparently someone somewhere
is giving orders

we could foresee the course of events
but were powerless to change them

the plan is the scientific instrument
of organisation of our victory

through self-criticism and emotionless
struggle we will eliminate bad thoughts

all thought must be reformed
in the depiction of reason and progress

the re-examination and revision of history
is a vital component

the continuation of the revolution
is perestroika, I have seen

much injustice in my life
I have become older and my fire quenched

while Lermontov's Masquerade is performed again
and dogs howl on the Nevsky Prospekt

and then there is the matter
of the Winter Palace wine cellars

there is no such thing as an absolutely hopeless situation
if the revolution is anything it must achieve goodness

look at the book, comrade
it is written in the book

The Pianist of Petrograd

Alas, alas that great city ... for in one hour is she made desolate

the clock you do not hear
strikes a time that cannot come

he predicted 1937
the most terrible year
he predicted 1939

what he felt as a boy
on the streets of Petrograd
was only a small prelude
to what will happen

you travel with the music
to a very mystical world
where millions of people don't want to be but
it's not their decision

he knew already that uninvited guest
death being most unwanted
can visit
anyone without exception

walking skeletons, people who are about to die
giving the symphony's premiere
in a big global space nothing
to do with propaganda

look for the music, don't look
for the political

branded formalist, cosmopolitan
comrades Shostakovich, Prokofiev
people don't need your music

people running, people shooting
it makes powerful sonorities
massive percussive signals

not as the guns or bombs
the falling buildings
or the cracking ice
but as Ravel's Bolero
that is how he hears war

perhaps I should write more slowly
and make fewer mistakes

I wanted to stay behind
and continue to create
but ran away to Leningrad
to hide with my mother

to lie down in hunger, to see
your loved ones starve
to wake with shuddering earth
and the sound
of gulls and crows
crying by the river

left hand crazy as a crossroads demon
dances across the keys

through bottle-heavy glasses he looks down
on devastated streets
patent leather shoes scuffing
the dust of paths that wind
between muddles of rubble and ash

On Suspicion of Sabotage in Project Planning

*Neither repented they of their murders, nor of their sorceries,
nor of their fornication, nor of their thefts*

the committee for language changes declares
this colourful symphony of reconstruction
a senseless product with a slavish
lack of clarity

how is it possible
for a person living in the world
to be in deliberate darkness
uninterested in revolution

where authorities control the lighting
a once conceivable love
stirs or may not stir
one more execution of the innocent

let us stop all reactionary criticism
and prevent certain church circles
from teaching our youth
how to commit murder

in the social war we need good laboratories
a spirit of defiance fills us and the city
but those who promise revolution
are frauds just like the others

the idea cannot be separated
from that of freedom
the front line is everywhere
there has never been so much

fucking in odd corners
yet the dead remain dead

The Utensil is Good But the Soup is Bad

And many men died of the waters, because they were made bitter

we've done all this just for this?
do you think congress could be mistaken
in error? let personal misfortune be bitter!
I see broken eggs, but if this is your omelette?

the scavengers know the price of ships
and shares girls and police chief – you think
you are driving the machine only
to find it is chasing you

we must throw all our energies into the fire
everything but our brains
from idle conveyor belts leather upholstery cut
tensile stretching rubber sole shoes

The House of the Gramophone Record, The House of the Book

> *Not to find one's way in a city ... requires ignorance, nothing more. But to lose oneself in a city, as one loses oneself in a forest, that calls for a quite different schooling.*
> —*Walter Benjamin*

everywhere new buildings display
the new dimensions and proportions
bridges now invest the river
with elegance and grandeur

ordinary events become hallucinatory
the inconceivable commonplace
the city is rapidly mutating, what were
old courtyards now filled

with eerily accurate maquettes
of monuments to be raised
buildings of extraordinary beauty
will line the glorious embankments

and high thoroughfares, newspapers
daily report the latest project
the newest opening, each addition
to the urban iconography

one faction demands that the city
be left untouched, the traitors
have been unmasked and dealt
an annihilating blow

the people's court convenes
an execution to be carried out with passion
the victim it is rumoured an official
in the ministry of culture

the people has spoken, the important point
the unnatural light of a lurid sky
of the kind that shines
on natural disaster

Expert Witness

Fear none of those things which thou shalt suffer: behold, the devil shall cast some of you into prison, that ye may be tried

in a trial against conspirators
there is no need of proofs
historical context
confirms the charges

the theatre of science and technology
plays continuously all day
to full houses of thirteen hundred seats
no one forgotten in the chorus

the production is better than the play
full as it is of heroic optimism
you must appreciate the implications of your guilt
the need for an enemy is immeasurable

the theatre for national minorities
must confirm the new canon
the presence of a jazz orchestra
is especially noteworthy

there is no cure for traitors
other than a gallows – or a lamp-post
coincidences and accidents
do not exist and yet

chance allocates to Piatokov
the role of judge or villain
to be executed – someone
must be accountable for catastrophes

unscrupulous regimes intensify
the fear of war and we are threatened

with a return to the time of confusions
falling to the work of defeatist elements

in the increasingly anonymous nature of dying
magicians and pimps have vanished from the register
the statistics are a crime that must be eliminated
along with the statisticians

From the Directory of 1936

Vladimir Antonov-Ovseenko, one of the leaders of the 1917 assault on the Winter Palace, was sentenced to death after being recalled from Spain in 1937

Leopold Averbach, General Secretary of the Association of Proletarian Authors, was denounced and shot in 1937

Gaston Bouley of the Commisariat of Foreign Affairs disappeared in 1937

YL Drobnis, democratic centralist, was shot in 1937

Francesco Ghezzi, Italian anarcho-syndicalist and union leader, disappeared in 1937

Golodiev, local government leader in Belarus, was shot or committed suicide in 1937

Abraham Gotz, former Social-Revolutionary terrorist, a senior official in the finance ministry, was tortured and shot in Alma-Ata in 1937

Ilya Ionov, firebrand of 1919, was shot in 1937

Lazar Kaganovich of the People's Commissariat for Posts and Telegraphs, was condemned to death in 1937

M Kalmanovich, the People's Commissar for Plant and Animal Production, was condemned and executed in 1937

Lev Karakhan, Bolshevik participant in the October Revolution, Soviet negotiator at the Brest-Litovsk Treaty, ambassador to China, was shot without public trial in 1937

Yuri Kotziubinsky, refusing to make false confessions, was expelled and executed without trial in 1937

Ivan Kraval, statistician in charge of the census, was arrested and executed in 1937

Kreps, the head of International Social Publishing, disappeared in 1937

S Lobov, the People's Commissar for the Timber Industry, died shortly after his expulsion from the Party in 1937

V Mezhlauk was condemned to death after his arrest in 1937

Nesterov, of the Planning Commission of the Urals, was shot in 1937

Heinz Neumann, German Communist leader, took refuge in the Soviet Union after the rise to power of Nazism and perished in 1937

Conservationist Vladimir Nevskii, who tried to preserve the Kremlin monasteries, was arrested in 1935 and shot in 1937

The former anarchist Novomirsky, a high official in the International, devoted himself to scientific work until he disappeared, with his wife, into a concentration camp in 1937

G Ordzhonikidze, the People's Commissar for Heavy Industry, committed suicide in 1937

Professor Pashukanis, director of the Institute for State and Law, was sentenced to death in 1937

Iurii Piatakov, deputy to Odzhonikidze, was sentenced to death in 1937

Novelist Boris Andreyevich Pilnyak was arrested without trial, removed to the Lubyanka and killed with a single bullet to the back of the head in October 1937

S Rataichak of the People's Commissariat was accused and shot in 1937

In 1926 the Right tendency within the Central Committee consisted of Rykov, Kalinin, Chubar, Petrovsky, Melnichansky and Dogadov; all but Kalinin perished in 1937

Arkadii Rozengol'ts, the People's Commissar for Foreign Trade, was sentenced to death after his arrest in 1937

Ian Rudzutak of the Council of People's Commissars, was sentenced to death after his arrest in 1937

Rykov, the People's Commissar for Post and Telegraphs, was sentenced to death after his arrest in 1937

Sachs-Gladnev, an old Marxist scholar, timid and fastidious, disappeared in 1937

The former anarchist Herman Sandomirsky, student of Italian fascism, disappeared in 1937

Timofey Vladimirovich Sapronov, a Bolshevik from 1912, was sentenced to death and shot in 1937

Leonid Serebriakov, former metalworker and inhabitant of Imperial prisons, soldier for the Revolution, organiser of the Railwaymen's Union, was shot in 1937

A Serebrovskii, in the leading ranks of the People's Commissariat, was accused and shot in 1937

Sheboldayev of the Central Committee was shot in 1937

What do our petty deportations amount to? said Smilga, who disappeared into jail in 1932 and died there in 1937

Artur Stashevskii, economic attaché in Spain, disappeared in 1937

Yan Sten of the Young Stalinist Left was shot around 1937

Geneticist N Vavilov of the Academy of Sciences died in prison after his arrest in 1937

I Veitser, the People's Commissar for Internal Trade, was executed after his arrest in 1937

Aveli Yenukidze, secretary since its foundation of the Central Soviet Executive, was shot without confession or trial in 1937

And Tonight the Hideous Angels Sue for Peace

the woods are full of images
of the young and middle-aged
new copies of old trial transcripts
cakes and apples and boiled sweets

absurd invented tokens
of remembrance adorn the trees
planted by secret police to conceal the graves
where soldiers threw the bodies
while the train was on the move

there are many unexpected things to explain
the irrationality of the epitaph
weird rhythms of lament
dust devils and bare earth
blurred figures against mist
the arrests and the shootings
did not stop for the war
in these days it is inconvenient to die

no day passes without a decree
but as yet there is no bread

Great Man Theory

*And there was given unto him a mouth speaking great things and blasphemies
… and power was given him over all kindreds, and tongues, and nations*

he does not flinch
as a fly
lands on his arm
then his forehead,
walks along his hairline,
settles finally on his eyeball

lays its eggs
in the pink inner corner
of the open lid
by the tearduct

any such thesis of the world
must account for
    Charlotte Corday
    Vera Zasulich
    Gavrilo Princip
    Nathuram Godse
    the headless torso of Danton
    the suspended form of Clara Petacci
    Hilde, Helga and Helmut
    Holde, Hedda and Heidi Goebbels
    poisoned by parents
    who could not let them outlive them

Mussolini's corpse, hung upside down
from the Esso station roof
stiffened with arms stretched
pushed back against the closing coffin lid
in imperial salute
or both arms raised

in oratorial acceptance
of acclaim

Lenin, on tour to the faithful
takes on an unwholesome pallor
green mould grows
on the tips of his fingers
and the end of his nose

Say Some of Your Poems to Me Again, Comrade Poet

one winter here and already
you speak like a veteran
of quarries and snow
of workers in the forest lost
in sudden drifts

you have your books
is that not enough?
you have candlelight
to write by and a fire
when we find the wood
it is surely better
than scratching a subsistence
among the peasants of the city

over coffee you will tell me
of the time of typhus and beheadings
how what was claimed in the morning
was often lost by dusk
how they felled him
in the middle of his song
the dangerous guitar silenced

lengthening shadows helped me
throw off spies on the street
we are political corpses
none but us left alive
and the lies we breathe in with the air

we are at the dark crossroads
history will summon us in time
like trainloads of the deported
leaving for the north, the forests

steppes, deserts
the statisticians jailed
and shot and still you believe
you are driving the machine

it was dawn at the edge of a clearing
they say, when Gumilev fell
his cap pulled down over his eyes
a cigarette hanging from his lips
showing the calm he had expressed
in one of his poems from Ethiopia

evening, when the street
is full of lights and working girls
brings the sense of defeat
and with it the inevitability of massacre
quite possible from week to week –
the front line is everywhere
out in the scrublands and marshes you will die
just as soon as in the library
with your perilous books

Joffe had no doubt his death
might be more useful
than to extend his life
in the genial malice
of this time of transition
all that now exists
of the commune state we dreamed of
is a beautiful hypothesis
a testament so toxic
that to read it is a crime

we are close to all the victims
and rebels of the world
the approaching era inescapable
the executioners schedule

themselves for execution
worthy of preservation for research

the old believers proclaim
the end of the world
panic so subtly contagious
that those who still have courage
are left only one option –

I felt no fear nor was I afraid
to show fear but even intelligent heroics
appear absurd wrapped
in near fatal spirit of defiance

the committees debate the question
of funeral rites – suicide remains
an act of indiscipline
there can be no question
of free speech until our perils are resolved

should we make an exception of a poet
and afterwards still shoot the others?
you may purify yourself with worthy novels
but the revolution still needs cash

poets and novelists are not political beings
they are not essentially rational
the intellectuals always are arrested
under whatever regime
just before the first of May

we saw the cracks in the earth widen
and were called seers
and so will stay
clinging to our last hopes
but can one lay down in advance
the date of a revolution?

after the massacre we met men
more stoical and anonymous
the anarchists too are wonderful
but an ideology fit for 12-year-olds

let us not be embittered
by the fates of individuals
or seek comrades of the firing squad
to learn how our friend
passed his final moments

in such times personal doubts
about the odd arrest seem very trivial
we speak of our sick party
but what else is there in the world?

it is in the nature of risings to end
in disillusion and disappointment
we know the downfall comes
when the revolution begins
to devour its own
the only hope of safety lies
in turning traitor swiftly enough –
if the state confiscates the grain
what is the point of sowing?

in deliberate darkness
where authorities control the lighting
a once conceivable love
stirs or may not stir

the dead still dead
the murderers proven
guilty but still free
one of the executed still alive

The Passing of Boris Pasternak

it is not necessary to start at the beginning
and always to reach the same end
by the same route

instead of a propensity to plan
we should endeavour always
to experiment and improvise

to bear witness to the impossible
the retrieval of the past in an age
that has outlawed history

one should not assume something
so advanced can only be reached
at what we would call the end of development

even in the most difficult of times
there are choices to be made
and doubt can make you more certain

we must not lick all the paint
off our gods – it is easier
to save a manuscript than a man

to stop the world from ending
we must spend time with exiles
in the gentle violation of taboos

this is the end of me but you live on
the complaining wind
rocks the house and the forest

don't forget tomorrow
to open the window

The penultimate stanza is adapted from one of Pasternak's Zhivago *poems, 'The Wind'; the last words are those of Pasternak himself; the sixth stanza incorporates a quotation from Nadezhda Mandelstam.*

II

From the Aesthetics Bureau

Document 1

everything has been deciphered:
language breaks down at the borders
of time and geography
art is not genetically determined

we try to respond
to interesting events
while mysterious mechanics maintain
aerial vigilance and a fleet

of throbbing harbingers
of deaths securely elsewhere
the blackbird and the chaffinch call
in the shrubbery dawn

small explosions shift the snow around
the painting took 12 years to restore
reflections on the surface
of a summer's day

blue lights shining above desert mountains
in the fuzz and blur of interference
an engineered crater 500ft deep
covered with blue film

children in shirts advertising bygone sponsors
pick through the components of old TV sets
seeking elements exchangeable
for canned goods and clean water

I am not so much interested in technical innovations
– buses, telegraph, electricity –
as in the more important questions
former people and careerists

to whom things happen
that they cannot explain
lavish funerals occurring
at times of change and uncertainty

young men of unknown occupation
and indeterminate appearance
have found out all there is to know
even a poet is motivated
by his sense of duty as a citizen

no one can say for certain
whether those figures are real or imagined
(glancing around occasionally
as if afraid of being overheard
they seemed to be speaking total nonsense:

'he is not just a foreign tourist
but a spy and a murderer'
– show me your papers
come with me for a few minutes
we need you simply to sign something)

cannibalised cars are piled up
museum quality classics
bashed and crazed
stripped to their chassis and bearings

this sad decay
in the house of ragged memory

carious teeth scuttle like spiders
through the dark margin
of the under-bed world

for a man with one grey suit
Shanghai in 1928 was no featherbed

his corner of the embassy
full of vials, chemicals and inks
photographic apparatus and codes

childlike, ageless as if he'd forgotten
his real name in all the changing
of nation and identity
but what is a person's *real* name?

De Wolff came down
like a Syrian upon the fold
the archbishop is glimpsed
burning redundant charters

he too had lost manuscripts
during searches of his apartment

the work of art withheld
is its own eloquence
the sentence must earn
its own truth

submarine and subliminal forces
never know whether or not
they are being detected

this sudden interlude of summer
striking hard against the old cold
catches us off guard
a rising damp of belly and legs
among logical dreams

from Sumer to Kursk the magical potential
of creative artillery has launched
shock and wonder
                      a shift of outlook
immense bearded figures of warlords

raised to strike terror
impose masculine
autocracy
          supporting civilisations
much later in distant lands
or subsisting in deserts until blasted
to kingdoms come and gone
by succeeding generations
of the historically
arrogant and mad

why should you help us expand
                            opening
factories and gun stores?

open the charms bar –
fear assumes different forms
history offers only
the most unreliable guide
we don't believe
in triviality
          least of all our own
everything profound loves a mask

like motes caught in rays by a window
cosmic dust becomes discernible to astronomers
by modulating the light passing through it
shockwaves of molecular hydrogen
and other revelations of character

occasionally the lava lake explodes
if there's no wind it's gorgeous
there is a wilderness here
or perhaps just a wildness

telltale dials show quantities in space and colour
petrified remains of long-extinct creatures
resemble politicians clustered round the pool

impressions of shellfish and seaweed trapped long ago
in mud hardened to rock
a cycle of sea transgressions and emerging land
shelly limestone dense
with brachiopods, crinoids, sponges, molluscs and corals

hammers and powerdrills of Isis assail
Ozymandias
          queen goddess bringing
an upstart rival down to size

Elizabeth I, refusing to give ground
stands upright three days in place
until finally compelled by approaching death
to sign away oil rights
and recline on the sophy's divan

at the summer fair our young goddesses
remain uncrowned
          dancing
round English maypoles
Kalashnikovs at the ready

classical authors tell how petrified remains
of unknown creatures were revealed
by erosion, storms, floods, earthquakes and digging

Greeks journeyed to view the bones
of beasts never seen alive
the insights were often expressed in mythological terms
teleological or aleatory creation

from bleak streets under bridges
to waterfront developments and
casual cliffs
          spurge and thrift
blowing in the cracks

protective clothing's necessary
masks to filter breathable air
latex gloves to ward against
the spurt of blood and pus

let's talk some more
about that mythology

the hunt for unclaimed bones
beneath a helicopter sky
organic shapes of weary form
a child's fur-grimed toy
snared in a hedge
Aristotle's silence on all this is bewildering

take up your treasure
and press it to your lips
for the simple pleasure
                            of communing
with anything of consequence

cargo-cultic figures
watch shyly from the edge
of the woods
            the clearing
where the provisioning planes
never come

like an eye
blinking at us
in the night

land forced into lateral slippage
and what becomes
of the dwellers there

all is nothing but illusion
contrived for the likes of us

all that really matters is missing

Leica Rangefinder, 50mm

how did it come to this?
strange things happen in markets
the adverbs and adjectives accumulate
and walls have a structuring effect

children playing around rubble
clambering among pretty dusty people
boys frolicking naked on cracked earth
while girls with plaits sell fruit

the first business of philosophy is to account
for things as they are
the art of war and revolution
when the rhythm is quickening

a sensation occasioned
by such recurring images
a portrait of a woman sobbing
in the remains of a building

a child crying in a crowd in rags
a kiss mistaken for a gunshot
furtive glee of a man on the run
beautiful women glimpsed from behind

geometric lives and ghostly rooms –
from such small deliverances
the passengers arrive
clutching their lovely things

what exactly is a decisive moment?
these dark tints are really in the picture
low-resolution messages to be glanced at
small gestures of humanity in the street

we infer the future from data about the past
like a dream of meaning
a badly crafted lie
breeding unnatural diseases

malign under the microscope
energy and absurdity
inconvenience mud and flies
the exacerbation of colour

I Could Tell You But Then
You Would Have to Be Destroyed

> *We've got to spend time in the shadows*
> —*Dick Cheney*

a plain photo of the outer wall
the interior roofline
a dun-coloured hill behind

what power lies
in keeping this secret
invisible

the men and women who carry out the program
are issued with fake identities
like subsidiary arms of a great company

unconvincing fluctuating signatures
of people who don't exist
officially

a base in the desert
for prisoners and drones
in easy range

of the most famous site
of casino, boxing ring
and glamour cabaret

suburban offices, middle-
aged men getting into cars
shimmering lines in the sky

aircraft waiting
to show us ourselves
in lives we are ignorant of

a black budget whose goal
is silence, listening
to what we do not know

existence inferred
from influence exerted
in obscurity

from blank spots on the map
bland blurring of
the satellite image

a very traditional British landscape
rolling hills and little stone houses
the surveillance base is just another element

it is the place they call the Salt Pit,
a goatherd wearing
a Dick Cheney baseball cap

pagodas that are not pagodas
on a strip of barren shingle
off-limits except to the sea

Monochromatic

what mama wore
and whether I loved her

her jowly frown
her big black blouse

the barn that was then
not yet deserted and her old

face half-reflected
in the dusty window

of a car and outside
the world blurs by

fenceposts and corn
maybe mere scrubland

her scarf appears green
in the black-and-white image

Visiting Time

memories depart
like unscheduled trains
going where they shouldn't go

you speak through a kind of box
and a glass partition smeared
with the semen of strangers

frequencies divide
choice and compensation
there's a lag and we get it late

days to get the stench
of the maggot factory
from clothes and nostrils

black-and-white photographs
of childhood cancer
behind her on the shelf

papers inherited
with the house
and the sense of shame

Bleed

the yak-driver must know
where to drive his blade
to tap the rich flow from the artery
drunk from the living neck
or turning the milk lilac
in life-giving warmth

people of the stone tower culture
seek communion with their god
in drinking his blood
identified spectrally
in red shift spectroscopy
the moment of (pro)creation
receding forever in astronomic time

in this space
a drop of poppy seed
stands for the act of war
sousing fallow farmland in
a bodily fluid blue until spilt

Purity

limpieza de sangre is of crucial
import since the taint
may cast discredit
on the loftiest
rooted inferiority
meaning the absence of
particular forebears
the libelled expelled
or put to death
for supposed writings

among the smaller community
of eternally tarnished blood
his wife touched the inmost
recesses of his life
for ritual purposes
blaming it on fanatics
and a statute of 1804
locking peoples in
perpetual conflict
physically degenerate
deceitful and exploiters

not forgetting to plunder
the abominated
by mass assimilation
moans within the earth
and seeping squirting
for the protection of honour
an account presented
to the present day
forbidding relations
beyond the war's veil
and the settlement

On Prenzlauer Allee

whose legs are these
laid out knee to knee
in the lit window?

imagine your own thigh
in that near sheer hose
her ankle in the rumpled sock

gaze face hidden
or the boot you might
walk out in stamped

with your own authority
and the gleam behind the glaze

Child #98

the blind gaze
of a detached head

face and hair painted
on broken eggshell

deformed feet overlong
articulated metal toes

protruding from flesh
of dirty beige stockinette

phallic extension of neck
where the head might hang

bearing the number
and importer's stamp

Roberson and Co 99 Long Acre
a luggage label attached like a noose

with a knotted
bootlace once white

frayed twine wadding shows
through worn elbows

upper arms and contorted
fingers and hands

Parisian-stuffed for muscles
seam up the spine

oval holes at the shoulderblades
buttonhole stitched

exposed screw-heads
at the wrists and groin

mannequins contain both
natural materials and worked metals

invite disturbing speculation
on docility of children

a fractured left knee joint noted
a human analogue

one headless adult four children
with two damaged heads

a recession from which
they never fully recovered

the artificial figure is
the most direct route to realism

a bunker off Brooklands Avenue
expresses its concrete function

the system of emergency
government restructured

being in the presence of a lifesize
being in which life is not

absent but in abeyance
a blank screen for desire

the dreamer who falls
in love with

a tailor's dummy a man
without a face

men make models
of women the result

so much more real
doubly silenced

embodying the gaze
mouths full

developments in robotics
living dolls and golems

rugged wooden boxes
with twisted rope handles

the secretive state extends
this invitation

a fine selection of genuine
prints and old maps

fakes in states
of slo-mo decomposition

we see words we see pictures
construct shapes

reading involves visual
sectors of the brain

texts are not simply transparent
bearers of content

not all of these processes are involved
in working out meaning

time here goes so quickly
you don't need to say keep still

Vision of Ezekiel
David Bomberg, 1912

a shock of tubular limbs shining in revolt
    explosive renewal of a machine age
        the rapture looks oddly like lamentation
            in death or resurrection the people have lost all identity
                no sinews come upon them

        the sacrificial calf's
      effaced as the geometric play of metal bones
    contending in mathematic fantasy
charismatic in stop-frame

— son of man, can these bones live?

kneeling in abasement or jubilation
    grappling in combat or physical affection
        an ecstasy of falling or a wrestling throw
            judged by gesticulating spectators

        there are things to be planted, written down, thrown off
      like faith, flesh, all language but the bodily
    dispatched beyond the apex and its corollary
like slaves, mothers and the solitary child
    upheld, outreaching, tossed to the tumult
        in hard layered light of late evening or dawn

        and what goes on beyond the unremitting frame
      congress of chaos on a raised dais
  a pool, a playground, a guarded compound
marketplace, temple and boxing ring
    sales floor and ritual bath
        attendants pointing beyond delineated spaces
            of and out of the crowded city

        in shades of pink and blue the river
      of light's a conveyor
    on which we recline, resigned
to the repetition of folly

– behold, they said, our bones are dried
and our hope is lost

  a battlefield, a hilltop, a stage
    with watchers overwhelmed or indifferent
      by a railway track to nowhere and back
        parts and particles locked in a framework
          beyond the moat, the haha, the pit

    the surprised dead rising
    from sepulchre and tiered ground
   to existence without ipseity
bones come together, bone to his bone

bodies caustic and eruptive from the ruled structure of the podium
    step up and bend to the evocation of enigmatic emotion
      Ezekiel on the Mound of the Deluge
        prophesying fall and rise
          figuratively strong

De Triomf van de Dood
Pieter Bruegel the elder, 1562

starved and starving dogs of death
   scavenge on the flesh stripped
     from the dead and dying
       bent backed, intent

on making what they will
   of folly's bounty
     beneath the domes of the catacombs
       skeletons stacked

awaiting resurrection
   monks and priests whose meat
     once adorned
       femurs, metatarsals and sockets

heaped up in niche upon niche
   faith and distrust misplaced
     replacing theology with radioactivity
       sub-alpha particles with god

the omniscient system that shapes
   eternal interlocking connections
     the dead will advance
       from the earth

to cudgel and lash the living
   punish their squalid misery and sin
     the dead in shrouds and windingsheets
       regimented on horseback

playing the hurdy-gurdy
   with dead-eyed rush-hour faces
     in rust brown fields
       with hose and snake and fire

the naked man pursed by starving hounds
    the dying at their gaming board
        the dead tolling bells
            the ship of fools sailing

from a smokesmeared horizon
    crows attending carrion
        on the gallows
            gaunt dogs nibble the baby

at the dead mother's fallen breast
    hellhounds, boneyard hounds, ossuary curs
        plagued by tumour and cancer
            cankers, lesions, rotting sores

the dead whose heads
    protrude from their own arses
        the dead weighed
            in scales of injustice

the dead clothed in nothing
    but their crowns and insignia
        the dead who once were
            glorious as you are now

the emaciated dead beating kettledrums
    pouring lees from wineskins
        the skeletal dead triumphant
            waving banners over the field

where broadsword and H-bomb
    halberd and napalm and agent orange
        sarin, scud and ballista
            rampage and crossbow

have done their work
    on a land stripped bare

    of crop and dwelling
        as a coin is found in a field

bearing the outward face
    of a forgotten tyrant
        of a forgotten dynasty
            and a people whose borders

are become obscure
    while the lights and pyres
        the fuel rods and flares
            that forged this power

continue to decay underground –
    you will say the soil in this garden
        is malnourished, unprepared
            for the weight of intent

it must uphold
    but the songs and sounds
        of bush and scrub
            the sparse vegetable patch

landscape scars
    and parched, toxic well
        must bear all the meanings
            we still have to face

The Garden of Earthly Delights

an imperial measure
under a burning sky
before the fall
           gates guarded
by gunwielding boys
pink knees below khaki shorts

here in Paradise Palestinian women
drink coffee and contemplate
the perfect morning
                tired groups
on the ship King Carol are homeless Jews
barred from entering by the quota system

for two months they have wandered
seeking land where they would be permitted
until finally Poland consented

in order to destroy the strongholds
and hiding places of Arab rioters
British troops are detailed
to dynamite older portions of the city
the demolition
            clears the way
for the building of new roads
others are posted throughout the town
to deal with the hostile demonstrations
of the evicted
            funds are raised in Nablus
to rebuild obliterated structures

due to the continued hostilities
Jewish police are trained
by British officers

                        whose authorities
have taken over the railways
special arrangements made
to guard the line
                        owing to the secret entry
of rebels from Syria and the Lebanon
strict watch must be kept
by the French and British police
under the ancient gates
and Mohammedan mosques
at the frontier

                        throughout July
colonists and Arab bands
have engaged in clashes
with often fatal results
during the present troubles
volunteer soldiers are kept busy
preventing interference
                        with the colonies
trucks of British soldiers are seen
on the road to ancient Hebron
new rubber-tyred British
3.75 howitzers bombarding
rebels in Galilee
                modern
American style skyscrapers
office buildings and apartment houses
finely paved wide streets
and smart shops show
the remarkable growth
of the New Jerusalem
                        Arab landowners
have profited largely
from the growth
                of the holy city
from a mere
                medieval village

Unified Field Theory

The most incomprehensible thing about the universe is that it is comprehensible
　　　　　　　　　　　—Albert Einstein

Tell all the truth but tell it slant
　　　　　　　　—Emily Dickinson

the soldier is walking in the city
foreigners and journalists if allowed to visit
are accompanied by guards
please take your seats in the theatre
a closed meeting is about to begin

the moose's head is not a moose's head
it is a fake fur hat that lies at a comedy angle
on top of a pile of old clothes
by the peeling radiator
in the underground kitchen

like you it has little prospect of leaving
it would not be fit for life in a larger world
the wall is not to make us close-minded
or isolated but to provide us special status
to guard things that are useless
while things that are valuable are left unattended

Zarechny is full of out-of-bounds areas
notably Rosatom a state-owned corporation
making parts for nuclear weapons
photography is banned there
two-thirds of employees don't care
what ideology prevails
and many men died of the waters
because they were made bitter

in the airconditioned atrium
beneath the immigration department

the fervour on my Facebook feed grows
and the live streams of trials stop
the wheel and the wing-petal
an accelerating cavity
corrupted by religion
sentiment and frivolity
pre-Newtonian explanations of gravity
mysterious drive-by shootings
and rocket attacks

your merchants were the great
men of the earth for by your
sorceries were all nations deceived
it is nothing to do with her hands
the lines and cracks there
white crescents of cuticle
the availability and economy of the pocket
unseamed opened out unsent envelopes
unspoken hazards

our intentions are pure and we remain transparent
engaging with the ambiguous world
the relativity of human knowledge
learning to recognise rocks wildlife and stars
the abiding necessity of art
provisionality and deferred meaning
all the manuscript variants rising
from the sacred site of the archive

nothing is affected by being known
the form of a constellation
can be construed only from elsewhere
a campaign of civil disobedience
quelled with bullets
by order of the national council for peace
let us choose good people
to produce the plane upon which
different things may enter into relation

between the lake and the pathway
watched by eyes of hawk and boar
a high structure of ivy
leafy and luxurious
may conceal at its dark heart
a brick tower a rotted tree
or an abandoned corner
of concrete stone or steel
a metaphor may also be a physical thing

the evidence is difficult to interpret
it is different from the debris of daily tasks
points produced from coloured stones
deliberately broken on site
decorative incised similarity
appears on pieces of red ochre
rockets land and perforated
beads worn as ornament
pigments as paint and pastel
have no practical explanation
these novel features
unrelated to hunting or climatic change

an envelope refolds discreetly
even after it has been sliced completely open
the light of the constellation
is of several different ages
synaptic responses produced by
food sex and defence
culture language and technology
the figurative ape forms the axe
consistency of its symmetry and shape
overlaps with the activity of expression
sharing food and bonding
through music and the print on the wall

the battery that powers it
is a sophisticated prefrontal cortex

an engine of thought through symbols
of images and words
made of bone or antler
and small firms ivory and stone
sculpture drawing and designs numerous
intentionally placed in the pit of custody outside

points signs and red lines
contours of bears and other animals appear
in the light of the fire as your ears
strain for extraneous sounds
knowing the silence and inscriptions
the assimiliated voltage of monsters
not yet domesticated or intimidated
the present modernity of horses
in a window by Chagall

at first it was just the Thing
a reification fetishising the weird
and novel object that could blow
apart a city reconfigure the molecules
of a million lives and their livers
as dangerous dismembered disfigured
disintegral dust

invading or defending territory
marauding Saxons or Dragoons
occupy the ground between the brickworks
and the power station steaming gently in
the autumn sun the roiling sea
penetrates subterranean fissures moisturising
acres of farmland threatening dissolution
of the hidden portion of high structures

alas that great city
for in one hour is she made desolate
the king will be brought down

as will the steepling minarets
of cardinals popes and ministers
of highest finance
teetering on vertiginous brinks
like spent fuel rods
as tides turn with the moon

blood from the bull's neck thick and warm
the wound already healing
chiselled faces painted red ochre and tan
screamface masks for gatecrashing rides of joy
real or fake what difference?
bricks hurled in staged anger
or ersatz glee bottled
up urine unthrown preserved for veneration

nothing that is said here leaves this room
but what a hazard a letter is
scented perhaps unsent
such little miscommunications
neurology as a source of authority
engaging with the ambiguous world
flatbed trucks over greasy plains
dingy containers for airline foods
beauty lies in the refusal of meaning
bakelite dials and twitching needles
naked electrodes in the kommandant's cell

a transition radiation tracker wheel
under silicon petals drives
the engine of false realities
residents make holes in the wall
where ongoing reform might one day open their city

American liberals believe the lies of economic peace
as the planes roar home
or so we're told

their contrails trailing glory
avoiding the sludge of meaningless compassion
or just going down
in a blaze watched
by quietened children

nature becomes a synonym
for suffering and death

in the dreary round
of swinging tree to tree
rooftop to rooftop
this careful camera
angle to that

local officials cast the migrants out
starvelings burning with fevers and pox
their mission to disappear
in clichés of climatic determinism
washed on the shores
of a Greek island lovely with myth

News of the World

a dark of your own fabulation
iron-walled
earth-lined
secret intelligence comes only
in laughter from distant caverns
or rumoured voices
words reduced to tones
which may not be believed

they say there is war
they say there is peace
poverty / prosperity
victory / defeat
they say all around is protest
hunger and plenty

they say walls have been torn down
but not this one
they say nothing at all
is written on the river
understandings of elsewhere
hummed on the wires
in the head
in the dark
means only what it means
and that is nothing

To Answer a Different Question Than the One Asked

languaged like this
there are things samizdat will not speak of
how we weep
only with people we like

drink our own home-brewed vodka
with added caesium and strontium
a wonderful evening
just like old times

let me put it this way
I still remember
the beautiful crackling
of the shortwave radio

voice of America
or perhaps the BBC
before the uncomfortable things emerged
like the complete works of Lenin

offloaded at the recycling centre
party cards on sale as souvenirs
among the matryoshki
icons and portraits of the tsar

Hut

nobody speaks
of what takes place
in the white hut
by the railway siding
the smell of old oil
and human waste

III

Stories About the Wind

In the Operations Room

vigilant, homed under water,
we find a bug in the game
to get the drones
to work together

with the capabilities
of amplified intelligence
from rival powers dealing
with incidents under pressure

the key mission
of the system of systems
is prediction, a continuum
of security threats pursued

a mesh of subtle algorithms
has eliminated false alarms
patterns of vulnerability
written into the language set

unseeable behind the high wall
the invisible border fencing
microwave insignia barring
the faceless unnamed

our facebook liking burned
into their fingertips and eyeballs
leaving their blood
uncoded on the waters

Ghosts

wooden beams of the temple halls
flexed and groaned by weight of water

he saw the wreckage, saw the sea
the buildings damaged, woods displaced
corpses and boats on the rooftops of ruins

at darkness figures passed the house
parents and children, a grandfather and child
covered in mud, staring
like people known or seen before
somewhere

this one had not drowned as most had
but died of a blow to the chest
from some big piece of rubble

families light candles and lanterns
to welcome the ancestors home –
who now is to fulfil the contract
between the survivors and the dead?

all around you dogs
bark too loudly to bear
give them rice to eat and water
let them in, hear their story

Test Site III

and illuminates the world
gleam entering the body
the smell of its substance
plane blacked out
in spurious protection
flying blind into the glow
flash dancing in the bone

then when the shock wave hits
pummelled up another 200 feet
aircraft of such tonnage
acting like a leaf
on a blowy night
thermal curtains flying
big eyes unclosed
earth heaving and popping
old paint under a blowtorch

and a small private army
bought secondhand
stacking used engines
batteries and fuselage
wings torn off by sordid boys

we sort the plastic from each other
bundle unread newsprint
warheads past their use-by date
spent fuel rods and radiant cones
measureless buried in closely
where they will or will not
go off or leach half-lives
into a soil washed by wavelets
on unforbidden shore

and the poets of the old nations
told stories about the wind
and the planes come sparking
out of the mountains

and she paces the floor
and wants to teach fear
a sudden windshift
rumours associated with
bureaucratic detail
the bedding the canned food

lighting of the morgue
drawings pinned by the blackboard
in a schoolroom entered
by metal ladder
beneath a concrete cover in a shaft

Krasnogorskiy

water comes frozen home in metal churn
hand-drawn on a wooden sled
shadows on linen-white snow
taller than the house
its regimental blue-framed windows
no higher than the satellite dish
behind the picket fence
for telephone connectivity
where Raisa has nursed her husband
through two bouts of the sickness

after this slumber my blood
began rising for no reason
headaches beyond the word
affects your mentality
on edge of nausea and memory loss

the mine now a ruin
six-storey living blocks
in concrete geometry
tumbled at the corner
under weight of snow
the bared walls' colour
matching that of the sky

we have some doubts
the village has an odd place
and strange weather patterns are often forced
to go smoke chimney down instead of up
so many sent their children
to other towns
I live on this street for 60 years
now where will they send?

a few dozen families remain
where thousands worked
uranium from the hard earth
in another country
another political time

sometimes I think they know the reason
and they are doing this
to drive us from this place
in voluntary resettlement
to re-establish some remote area
I saw a house they offer

I do not want
to live in such condition

* * * *

you cannot see from here the human pelts
the traffic in the cities and the trade in lives
you cannot see the purpose of the power
dug out of the ground round here

you cannot see from here the rocket launch site
raised to rain destruction on far lands
now flinging into orbit satellites
for the navigation of family cars and vans

* * * *

my brain switched off
that's it, I don't remember
I understood on waking
that I'd fallen asleep

I saw my daughter's delirium
and you do not want it again
Margarita was horrible hallucinations
looked at me and told
Mama, you have three eyes
and there's something
crawling on the radiator

* * * *

tests are ongoing
on the air, soil, water, food
animals, building materials
and the people themselves

the broken settlement
settling into the soil
homes of miners once dispatched
from the centre now a foreign land

a lack of scientific facts
led to suspicion of the mine
that fed its power to nuclear
weapons and energy plants

radiation is within permissible levels
and the concentration of heavy metal salts
elevated levels of radon
were ruled out as the cause

there are no reports
of similar occurrences in mining times
we don't have results
of the studies in our hands

some measures must be taken
this is a chance for the residents

of our village to find new homes
and new lives elsewhere

* * * *

Dear Karim, based on the above, please pay attention
to the situation in the village Kalachi and that to date
there is no clear conclusion of the authorized body
of the reasons that cause encephalopathy of unknown etiology
despite the large number of studies

meanwhile villagers notice the disease progresses
on warm days, currently new patients with symptoms
revealed three to four times a week
for almost two years, population one quarter of the village
the first patient admitted March 2013, today 64 sick

this paper indicates the working group has conducted
more than laboratory, instrumental and clinical studies:
soil, air, water, food, fodder, building materials,
indoor air, patients with this type of disease
as well as all residents have been examined

out of all the studied factors was noted in excess
of 37 per cent of homes the presence of radioactive gas – radon
(increased to seven times) also in cases of blood
with increased levels of carbon monoxide
in water samples exceeding the radon ration three times

disease studies involve specialists of state bodies, in particular
the former ministry of health and its three research centres
the national security committee, ministry of internal affairs,
national nuclear centre and the American centre for control
and prevention of infectious diseases

studies and disease create social tension
in the village and small town Krasnogorsk

where previously it was suggested demolition
but thus convinced Sergey Lukashenko
director of the institute of radiation safety:

that sleepy disease is not caused by radiation poisoning
although he's slightly elevated, my deep belief
we sweep aside this factor that cannot act, we sweep aside
almost a factor of exposure to heavy metals, this is also verified
in this case, according to measurements

* * * *

we have some suspicions
we are all in fear
of falling asleep
between hauling water
from the standpipe

and then she looked over my shoulder
and cried Mama
you have three eyes and something
is crawling on the radiator

Test Site IV: New Fire

> *And the prince smote the cities of his enemies with the new fire, and for three days and nights did his great catapults and metal birds rain wrath upon them. Over each city a sun appeared and was brighter than the sun of heaven, and immediately that city withered and melted as wax under the torch*
> —Walter M Miller Jnr, *A Canticle for Leibowitz*

we cross the harsh light of gravel flatlands
seeking our plastic souvenirs
a model missile silo kit for the kids

the Las Vegas Range is visible
a scored and crinkled backdrop
to the Red Eagles
parked on the tarmac
where the Gunsmoke gunnery
came into the world
and Aggressor pilots train
in the glow from The Strip

the launch sites are buried deep
safe from any blast except their own
grate-covered holes bear a warning:
toxic vapours

escape by miscalculation
tracked by government weathervanes
rattlers won't get past the blast doors
to the no lone zone

fully operational the B61-12
is a nuclear gravity bomb
the test flight employed
no highly enriched uranium
or plutonium, consistent
with test treaty obligations

in a demonstration of effective
end-to-end system performance

walkie-talkies are banned in the missile shaft
to stave off degradation of guidance
a long green catwalk suspended from above
in the lamplit cave of the silo

delivery was effected
by an F-15E from Nellis Air Force Base
in a realistic guided environment
all scheduled activities successful
telemetry and video data collected

we pass the pamphlets around at parties
delivering the ordnance with the canapés
someone unthinking asks
what happened to the guy
who dropped the ratchet on the rocket

here you may wait patiently
for a message that never comes

the upgrade is a dumb bomb
enhancing national security
through nuclear science
improved accuracy and lower yield
considered usable

targets and ballistic calculations
calibrated to a fine degree of death
unless your walkie-talkie fucks the guidance

Oshita-chan lived approximately
12 hours after pikadon

Select bibliography

Anne Applebaum, *Iron Curtain* (London 2012)
EH Carr, *The Russian Revolution from Lenin to Stalin 1917-1929* (London 1979)
Jackie Copleton, *A Dictionary of Mutual Understanding* (London 2015)
Don DeLillo, *Underworld* (New York 1997)
William Doyle, *The Oxford History of the French Revolution* (Oxford 1989)
Richard P Feynman, *Don't You Have Time to Think?* (London 2005)
Orlando Figes, *A People's Tragedy* (London 1996)
Sheila Fitzpatrick, *The Russian Revolution* (Oxford 2008)
Nikolai Gogol, *Dead Souls* (Boston 1886)
Geoffrey Hosking, *A History of the Soviet Union 1917-1991* (London 1985)
Samuel Iwry, *To Wear the Dust of War* (New York 2004)
Arthur Koestler, *Darkness at Noon* (London 1940)
Lionel Kochan, *Russia in Revolution* (London 1967)
W Bruce Lincoln, *In War's Dark Shadow* (New York 1983)
—— *Passage Through Armageddon* (New York 1986)
—— *Red Victory* (New York 1989)
Nadezhda Mandelstam, *Hope Against Hope* (New York 1970)
Catherine Merridale, *Night of Stone* (London 2000)
Alan Moorehead, *The Russian Revolution* (London 1958)
Boris Pasternak, *Doctor Zhivago* (London 1958)
Roger Pethybridge, ed, *Witnesses to the Russian Revolution* (New York 1967)
David Priestland, *The Red Flag* (London 2009)
Albert Rhys Williams, *Through the Russian Revolution* (New York 1921)
Karl Schlögel, *Moscow 1937* (Cambridge 2012)
Aidan Semmens, *The Book of Isaac* (Anderson, SC 2013)
Victor Serge, *Memoirs of a Revolutionary* (London 1963)
Year One of the Russian Revolution (London 1972)
Pitirim A Sorokin, *Leaves From a Russian Diary* (Boston 1950)
L Trotsky, *The History of the Russian Revolution to Brest-Litovsk* (London 1919)

Unattributed epigraphs are from *The Revelation of St John*, King James Version, 1611

www.ingramcontent.com/pod-product-compliance
Lightning Source LLC
Chambersburg PA
CBHW031159160426
43193CB00008B/439